Notes to Myself:

My struggle to become a person.

Hugh Prather

Other useful books from Real People Press:

EMBRACE TIGER, RETURN TO MOUNTAIN: the essence of T'ai Chi, by *Al Chung-liang Huang.* Huang learned T'ai Chi Chuan from many teachers—as a child in China, and later in Taiwan. In his teaching he reverses the traditional way and conveys the essence and process of T'ai Chi first, with the form (Chuan) coming in easily and naturally later. The essence of T'ai Chi is a way of living as well as a way of moving. This book is compiled from tapes of his workshops at Esalen and other growth centers and his university classes in dance. It includes some instruction in calligraphy and interpretation of the *Tao te Ching*, as well as showing how T'ai Chi can become a part of every facet of life. Illustrated. 185 pp. 1973 Cloth $7.00 Paper $3.50

AWARENESS, by *John Stevens,* Detailed instructions lead you through more than a hundred experiments in exploring your awareness of yourself, your surroundings, and your interaction with others. These experiments—based on Gestalt Therapy and developed in the classroom and in groups—give you actual experience with methods that you can use further, either as teacher, group leader, or on your own, to work through difficulties and get more in touch with your own flow of experiencing. 276 pp. 1971 Cloth $7.00 Paper $3.50

DON'T PUSH THE RIVER, by *Barry Stevens.* A first-person account of the author's use of Gestalt Therapy and the ways of Zen, Krishnamurti and the American Indian to deepen and expand personal experience and work through difficulties. "We have to turn ourselves upside down and reverse our approach to life." This autobiographical episode shows the author doing this during a three-month period in association with Fritz Perls at the Gestalt Institute of Canada in 1969. 280 pp. 1970 Cloth $7.00 Paper $3.50

GESTALT THERAPY VERBATIM, By *Frederick S. Perls.* The originator and developer of Gestalt Therapy gives a clear explanation in simple terms of the basic ideas underlying this method, which at the same time makes a contribution to existential philosophy. This is followed by verbatim transcripts of complete therapy sessions, with explanatory comments. 280 pp. 1969 Cloth $5.00 Paper $3.50

IN AND OUT THE GARBAGE PAIL, by *Frederick S. Perls.* A novel autobiography in which he applies his theory of focusing on awareness, and writes "whatever wants to be written." Partly in poetic form, often playful, sometimes theoretical, the book is a many-faceted mosaic of memories and reflections on his life—in the past and at the moment—and on the origins and continuing development of Gestalt Therapy. Illustrated. 280 pp. 1969 Cloth $7.00 Paper $4.00

PERSON TO PERSON, by *Carl Rogers and Barry Stevens.* Professional papers by Rogers and others—about therapy, experiencing and learning—are set in a matrix of personal response and the use that Barry Stevens has made of these papers in arriving at better understanding of herself, and her view of the problem of being human as she has encountered it in her life. 276 pp. 1967 Cloth $4.50 Paper $3.00

The name *Real People Press* indicates our purpose: to publish ideas and ways that a person can use independently to become more *real*—to further his own growth as a human being and to develop his relationships and communication with others.
12   13   14   15   16   17   18   19   20   21   22   23   24   25   printing
76   75   74   73

to
Carl Rogers
(whose *On Becoming A Person*
showed me where to look)

If I had only . . .
forgotten future greatness
and looked at the green things and the buildings
and reached out to those around me
and smelled the air
and ignored the forms and the self-styled obligations
and heard the rain on the roof
and put my arms around my wife
    . . . and it's not too late

She may die before morning. But I have
been with her for four years. Four years.
There is no way I could feel cheated if
I didn't have her for another day. I didn't
deserve her for one minute, God knows.

And I may die before morning.

What I must do is die now. I must
accept the justice of death and the
injustice of life. I have lived a good life—
longer than many, better than most. Tony
died when he was twenty. I have had
thirty-two years. I couldn't ask for
another day. What did I do to deserve
birth? It was a gift. I am *me*—that is a
miracle. I had no right to a single minute.
Some are given a single hour. And yet I
have had thirty-two years.

Few can choose when they will die. I
choose to accept death now. As of this
moment I give up my "right" to live.
And I give up my "right" to her life.

But it's morning. I have been given
another day. Another day to hear and read
and smell and walk and love and glory.
I am alive for another day.

I think of those who aren't.

Today I want to do things to be doing
them, not to be doing something else. I
do not want to do things to sell myself
on myself. I don't want to do nice things
for people so that I will be "nice."
I don't want to work to make money,
I want to work to work.

Today I don't want to live for,
I want to live.

My prayer is: I will be what I will be
and I will do what I will do.

All I want to do, need to do, is stay in
rhythm with myself. All I want is to do
what I do and not try to do what I
don't do. Just do what I do. Just keep
pace with myself. Just be what I will be.

"I will be what I will be"—but I am *now*
what I am, and here is where I will
spend my energy. I need all my energy to
be what I am today. Today I will work
in rhythm with myself and not with what
I "should be." And to work in rhythm
with myself I must keep tuned in to myself.

God revealed his name to Moses, and it
was: I AM WHAT I AM.

I am convinced that this anxiety running
through my life is the tension between
what I "should be" and what I am. My
anxiety does not come from thinking
about the future but from wanting to
control it. It seems to begin whenever I
smuggle an "I want to become" into my
mind. It is the tension between my desire
to control what I will be and the recognition
that I can't. "I will be what I will be"—
where is the anxiety in that? Anxiety is
the realization that I might not reach the
rung on the opinion-ladder which I have
just set for myself. I fear death most
when I am about to exceed what others
expect of me; then death threatens to
cut me off from myself, because
"myself" is not yet.

I can not "make my mark" for all time—
those concepts are mutually exclusive.
"Lasting effect" is a self-contradictory
term. Meaning does not exist in the
future and neither do I. Nothing will
have meaning "ultimately." Nothing will
even mean tomorrow what it did today.
Meaning changes with the context. *My*
meaningfulness is here. It is enough
that I am of value to someone today.
It is enough that I make a difference now.

"What do I want to do in life?" "What is my purpose?" My assumption is that I have a reason for living, that my life has a direction. But maybe we are not moving in one direction any more than history is. The assumption that I am headed toward something makes me want to justify my past actions and plan out (eliminate) the future. The reason I don't want to drive, wait in line, run errands, etc., is that in the back of my mind I believe I have a destiny and that therefore this mundane task is a waste of my time because it does not contribute to the "important work" I have to do before I die.

The way for me to live is to have no way. My only habit should be to have none. Because I did it this way before is sufficient reason not to do it this way today.

Time is change, therefore when I do something unfamiliar I literally consume more time per clock-hour. Familiar means less time because less change. Therefore I can lengthen my life by staying out of doctrines and ruts.

Confession is often an avoidance of
change. If I confess it, I don't have to
accept the responsibility of changing it:
"I confess. It is beyond my control."
And it shifts the burden: "You have heard
it, now what are *you* going to do about it?"

Why do I judge my day by how much I have "accomplished?"

When I get to where I can enjoy just lying on the rug picking up lint balls I will no longer be too ambitious.

I'm holding this cat in my arms so it can sleep, and what more is there.

After I had written this book I told
several friends. Their response was polite
and mild. Later I was able to tell them
the book was going to be published.
Almost to a man they used the words
"I am proud of you." Proud of the
results but not of the action.

Everyone but me looks *back* on my
behavior in judgement. They can only
see my acts coupled with their results.
But I act *now*. And I cannot know the
results. I give my actions their only
possible meaning for me, and this
meaning always issues from: "I am
responding to this part of me and
not to that part."

I don't live in a laboratory: I have no way of knowing what results my actions will have. To live my life for results would be to sentence myself to continuous frustration and to hang over my head the threat that death may at any moment make my having lived a waste. My only sure reward is *in* my actions and not from them. The quality of my reward is in the depth of my response, the centralness of the part of me I act from.

Because the results are unpredictable, no effort of mine is doomed to failure. And even a failure will not take the form I imagine. The most realistic attitude for me to have toward future consequences is "it will be interesting to see what happens." Excitement, dejection and boredom assume a knowledge of results that I cannot have.

If I work toward an end, meantime I am confined to a process.

The rainbow is more beautiful than the pot at the end of it, because the rainbow is now. And the pot never turns out to be quite what I expected.

★

je d'accord

There is a part of me that wants to write, a part that wants to theorize, a part that wants to sculpt, a part that wants to teach . . . To force myself into a single role, to decide to be just one thing in life, would kill off large parts of me. Rather, I recognize that I live now and only now, and I will do what I want to do *this* moment and not what I decided was best for me yesterday.

I say to people, "I always do so-and-so,"
or "I never do so-and-so," as if my
individualness depended on such
banal consistencies.

"Next time I will . . ."
"From now on I will . . ."
—What makes me think I am wiser today
than I will be tomorrow?

Boredom is useful to me when I notice it and think: Oh, I'm bored—there must be something else I want to be doing. In this way boredom acts as an initiator of originality by pushing me into new activities or new thoughts.

The more I consult my feelings during the day, tune in to myself to see if what I am doing is what I want to be doing, the less I *feel* at the end of the day that I have been wasting time.

I have recently noticed that many times each day I take a quick mental survey of my activities up to that point in the day in order to determine my direction. This mental activity is spontaneous, almost subconscious, and seems inherent. If my activities do not add up to a direction then I am at least slightly depressed and enervated. If for some reason I feel at that moment incapable of heading in a "good" direction then I sense a desire within me to head in a destructive direction: for example, to go, really *go*, to pot. Any direction seems decidedly preferable to no direction at all. This may be one of the causes of violence, destructive love affairs, alcoholism, etc. A "goal" is implied but the need seems to be for direction—to feel in the process of becoming.

As I look back on my life, one of the most constant and powerful things I have experienced within myself is the desire to be more than I am at the moment—an unwillingness to let myself remain where I am—a desire to increase the boundaries of myself—a desire to do more, learn more, express more—a desire to grow, improve, accomplish, expand. I used to interpret this inner push as meaning that there was some one thing out there I wanted to do or be or have. And I have spent too much of my life trying to find it. But now I know that this energy within me is seeking more than *the* mate or *the* profession or *the* religion, more even than pleasure or power or meaning. It is seeking out more of me; or better, it is, thank God, *flushing out* more of me.

The past is over and the future is not yet—my desires must therefore be in and for the present. "I hope I will lose some weight" means that right now I am experiencing a feeling of dissatisfaction because the reality of my body and the way I picture myself conflict. Thinking that my desires are for something in the future prevents me from accepting responsibility for them now, and worse, causes me to plan out my tomorrows.

Often the desires that I think are for the future are based on unrealistic concepts of myself that I want to fulfill. "I want to work out a theory of reality based on precognition"—is this a desire to be myself or a desire to fulfill some wishful image of myself? I am all that I am in the present. What I wish I were or think I ought to be has to be looked for in the future.

Perfectionism is slow death. If everything
were to turn out just like I would want
it to, just like I would plan for it to,
then I would never experience anything
new; my life would be an endless repetition
of stale successes. When I make a mistake
I experience something unexpected.

I sometimes react to making a mistake
as if I have betrayed myself. My fear of
making a mistake seems to be based on the
hidden assumption that I am potentially
perfect and that if I can just be very
careful I will not fall from heaven.
But a "mistake" is a declaration of the
way I *am*, a jolt to the way I intend, a
reminder I am not dealing with the facts.
When I have *listened* to my mistakes I
have grown.

When I see I am doing it wrong there is
a part of me that wants to keep on doing
it the same way anyway and even starts
looking for reasons to justify the continuation.

A sure way for me to have a disastrous experience is to do something because "it will be good for me."

ain't that the truth !

Just when I think I have learned the way
to live, life changes and I am left the
same as I began. The more things change
the more I am the same. It appears that
my life is a constant irony of maturity
and regression, but my sense of progress
is based on the illusion that things out
there are going to remain the same and
that, at last, I have gained a little control.
But there will never be means to ends,
only means. And I am means. I am
what I started with, and when it is all
over I will be all that is left of me.

There are occasions when I talk
to a man who is riding high on some
recent insight or triumph, and for the
moment life probably seems to him to
have no problems. But I just don't believe
that most people are living the smooth,
controlled, trouble-free existence that their
careful countenances and bland words
suggest. Today never hands me the same
thing twice and I believe that for most
everyone else life is also a mixture of
unsolved problems, ambiguous victories
and vague defeats—with very few moments
of clear peace. I never do seem to quite
get on top of it. My struggle with today
is worthwhile, but it is a struggle nonetheless
and one I will never finish.

i'm glad i'm not the only one who
feels like this

Possibly the greatest crime we commit
against each other is this daily show of
"normality." I have countless *little*
conversations with a variety of people,
and the impression I get is that most
men don't have problems. Even the
complainer presents himself as a victim.
He doesn't suggest that *he* is experiencing
confusion. He is all right: it is circumstances
which are bad.

The comment "Don't mind him, he's got
a problem" illustrates this universal attitude
toward personal difficulty. The implication
is that having a problem is a strange and
avoidable weakness. When I come in repeated
contact with this daily facade of normality
I begin to assume that I too deserve such
a life, and I get annoyed with the present
and look upon my difficulties as unjust
tragedies. And because I assume there is
something unnatural about my having a
problem, I attempt to present a problem-
free appearance too.

I live from one tentative conclusion to the next, thinking each one is final. The only thing I know for sure is that I am confused.

What an absurd amount of energy I have been wasting all my life trying to figure out how things "really are," when all the time they weren't.

Do I really think there is anything more profoundly true about my interpretation of the situation, now that I'm in bed, than there was when I was in the middle of it this afternoon?

There are no absolutes for something so relative as a human life.

For me, thinking seems to act at times as a defense mechanism, a way of avoiding some feeling, or a way of *not* looking at the situation I am in. I believe this is especially true in social situations, where I lead with my head.

My trouble is I analyze life instead of live it.

A theory is a theory, not a reality. All a theory can do is remind me of certain thoughts that were a part of my reality *then*. A statement or a "fact" is an emphasis—one way of looking at something. At worst it is a kind of myopia. A name is also just one way of seeing something. I can't make a statement about a reality without omitting many other things which are also true about it. Even if it were possible to say everything that is true about a reality, I still would not have the reality; I would only have the words. In fact, the reality changes even as I talk about it.

When I outgrow my names and facts and theories, or when reality leaves them behind, I become dead if I don't go on to new ways of seeing things.

I keep thinking I have to do something
to shore up reality. Bill and Leah are
over here—just let the conversation take
place. Don't push. Don't hang on. Lean
back and let reality happen.

I constrict my vision and disregard my
opportunities when I strive. I cannot
receive from the unknown when I grasp.
Nothing exists for me until I see it. There
is little I can do about my feelings, but
awareness removes the edge of myopia
from my wants.

Eloquence is sometimes lyrical, sometimes
powerful, but always an overstatement
and always a projection.

Dishonest people believe in words
rather than reality.

Anyone who inhabits himself cannot believe in objective thinking.

I reject objective thinking.

Now that I know I'm no wiser than anyone else, does this wisdom make me wiser?

The number of things just outside the perimeter of my financial reach remains constant no matter how much my financial condition improves. With each increase in my income a new perimeter forms and I experience the same relative sense of lack. I believe that I would be happy if only my earnings were increased by so much and I could then have or do these few things I can't quite afford, but when my income does increase I find I am still unhappy because from my new financial position I can now see a whole new set of things I don't have. The problem will be solved when I realize that happiness is a present attitude and not a future condition.

I don't need a "reason" to be happy. I don't have to consult the future to know how happy I feel now.

The comment, "You're lucky; it could have been worse," is the kind of "helpfulness" I can do without. It also could have been better, or actually, it couldn't have been any other way than the way it was.

At first I thought that to "be myself"
meant simply to act the way I feel. I
would ask myself a question such as,
"What do I want to say to this person?"
and very often the answer was surprisingly
negative. It seemed that when I looked
inside, the negative feelings were the ones
I noticed first. Possibly I noticed them
because of their social unusualness;
possibly they stood out because acting
negatively was what I feared. But I soon
found that behind most negative feelings
were deeper, more positive feelings—if I
held still long enough to look. The more
I attempted to "be me" the more "me's"
I found there were. I now see that "being
me" means acknowledging all that I feel
at the moment, and then taking responsibility
for my actions by consciously choosing
which level of my feelings I am going
to respond to.

When I first began trying to be myself,
I at times felt trapped by my feelings. I
thought that I was stuck with the feelings
I had, that I couldn't change them, and
shouldn't try to even if I could. I saw
many negative feelings inside me that I
didn't want, and yet I felt that I must
express them if I were going to be myself.

Since then I have realized that my
feelings do change and that I can have
a hand in changing them. They change
simply by my becoming aware of them.
When I acknowledge my feelings they
become more positive. And they change
when I express them. For example, if I
tell a man I don't like him, I usually like
him better.

The second thing I have realized is that
my not wanting to express a negative
feeling is a feeling in itself, a part of me,
and if I want *not* to express the negative
feeling more than I *do*, then I will be
acting more like myself by not expressing it.

Accept what is. That is what is required.
Accept reality as reality is to me *now*.
Recently I have been feeling anxious
about every little decision—what should I
wear?—what shouldn't I eat?—did I lock
the door?—am I worrying too much?
Right now this anxiety is my reality.

Don't fight a fact, deal with it.

The bully in me always bullies in the name of principle or in the name of rules. The bully in me always has a reason for its actions and that reason is always idealistic. This part of me is a sissy—it hides behind "what is right" so I won't have to admit my desire to hurt.

It seems that I have to get in touch with my desire to hurt *before* I can get in touch with my desire not to hurt.

Within me is the potential to commit
every evil act I see being committed by
other men, and unless I *feel* this potential
I can at any moment be controlled by
these same urges. I am free from these
urges only if I recognize when I am
feeling them, and while feeling them
and acknowledging them to be me, choose
not to follow them. Only in this way can
I begin to regain the disowned parts of me.
And only in this way can I know what it
is I am criticizing in others.

At times I want to hurt or intimidate
Moosewood. I especially feel this way
when she cowers. But when I am conscious
of these feelings and don't try to mentally
sidestep them but remain aware of
them and go ahead and flow with them,
then my feelings become more positive
and I play with her in a rough way she
enjoys. The awareness seems to transform
her in my mind. A second before, she
was an object to be kicked; now she is
my dog, with feelings, and I don't want
to hurt her.

If, on the other hand, I avoid my hurtful
feelings and don't identify them as part of
me, or even if I am aware of them but
battle them, then they become ugly. To
battle my feelings is to condemn myself
for having them and it's as if the condemned
part of me reacts by getting nasty.

Awareness, deep full awareness, always seems
to make my energy outflow more positive.

I am beginning to think that there are no
destructive feelings, only destructive acts,
and that my actions become destructive
only when I condemn and reject my feelings.
If I say that I don't want to feel a certain
way I disregard the fact that I *do* feel that
way and that the feeling is me. Feeling a
certain way is one feeling; not *wanting* to
feel that way is *another* feeling, and it does
not cause the first feeling to stop. I can
change my response to a feeling, but I can
no more get rid of it than I can get rid
of myself. When I disown a feeling I do
not destroy it, I only forfeit my capacity
to act it out as I wish. By condemning it
I stop believing it to be me and so it
seems to take on a life of its own and
force me to respond to it in a habitual
way. But if I see that *I feel the feeling*
then I retain my ability to act on it in the
way I choose rather than in the way I fear.

Tonight a little boy fell in my lap and
looked up at me for affection. I felt
tight and awkward. I was battling so hard
about how I "should" feel that I didn't
pause long enough to see how I *did* feel.
Maybe the fear that I didn't feel the love
I thought I should was groundless and
would have been there if I had not been
afraid to look at myself.

When Gayle gets sick I feel resentful, then angry, then nothing at all. I feel resentful: she's making a demand on me I can't fulfill (I can't quickly fix things up); she's using up my precious time; she's making a messy situation. Then I feel angry because I think I shouldn't feel resentful when someone is sick. Then I resign myself and my emotions shut down altogether. But if in the middle of this I pause long enough to look inside myself, I find that these negative feelings seem to be going on on the surface and that deeper within me are more positive, loving feelings. They are hard for me to stay in contact with under these circumstances and I lose them for certain if I try to act more sympathetic than I feel.

Unless I accept my faults I will most
certainly doubt my virtues.

If I truly accept my behavior
I no longer see it as a fault.

Both my body and my emotions were given to me and it is as futile for me to condemn myself for feeling scared, insecure, selfish or revengeful as it is for me to get mad at myself for the size of my feet. I am not responsible for my feelings, but for what I do with them.

It is equally as useless for me to be disgruntled about having had the thought I just had as it is for me to criticize myself for something I did last year. Okay, that is what I just thought—now *this* is what I'm thinking.

"You shouldn't feel that way." —My emotions do not originate in compliance with the laws of Aristotelian logic. My mind cannot know what my body "ought" to be feeling. My body has every reason of its own to be feeling the way it does, and all things considered (which my mind cannot do) it couldn't be feeling any other way.

"Don't condemn yourself for your feelings."

"Not even for the condemnatory ones?"

"Don't feel bad."

"But I *do*."

I feel what I feel what I feel.

I was just asked to go somewhere. I said,
"I can't. I have to stay home. Gayle's
sick." Clearly, I was not accepting
responsibility for my actions. Next time
I hope I have the courage to state that
I do what I do because *I* want to do it.

I notice sometimes I think, "I ought to
do so-and-so," in order to cover up my
desire to do it. If I "have" to do it I
don't have to admit I want to, or that I
don't want to.

The injunction to be unselfish is an
impossible ideal. Each of us is totally
selfish in the sense that we are always
doing what some part of us wants to.
Generosity feels at least as rewarding as greed.
Selfishness is neither inherently good nor
bad—it depends on the *way* we are selfish
as to whether it nourishes or injures.

i'm selfish —
it nourishes me ?
i hope it doesn't
injure you.

One kind of lie that I tell pops out in conversation and takes me by surprise. Sometimes I like to correct these lies right on the spot, and when I do I find that most people don't think less of me. This kind of lie, when I notice it, usually helps me to see where I feel inadequate—the areas where I could be more acceptant of myself.

Another kind of lie I tell begins when I think I can foresee the consequences of something I have done. I then start having fantasies about how I am going to explain things. I have noticed that if these fantasies go on unobserved they tend to convince a part of me that things happened more advantageously than they actually did, and I end up telling a lie—half believing it to be true. But if I become aware of these fantasies I can do something that interrupts this pattern: I can get very clear in my mind what did happen and what I would say if I wanted to tell the truth. I find that just doing this much sometimes takes a persistent effort. However, after doing this I usually *want* to tell the truth, and if I don't tell the truth I feel much better about lying.

When I examine my fantasies for the values
they express I am surprised at the pettiness.

Often my fantasies express how I would
like to feel rather than how I do feel.
Here's this man I'm afraid of and I
fantasize the part of the very tough person—
when actually I feel weak in relation to
him. Do I want to actualize myself? OK,
the actuality is I am afraid of him.

If I find I am afraid of getting beaten up I do not have to choose between either obeying the dictates of the fear or reacting against it; I have the alternative of acknowledging what I feel at the moment and allowing myself to do whatever grows out of that. Self-awareness increases my options, my range of choices.

Fear is static that prevents me from
hearing my intuition.

Anxiety, fear, panic, etc., is a fleeing
from something. There is something over
there in the corner of my mind, some
thought, some image, that I don't want to
look at, that I want to run away from.

Fear is often an indication I am avoiding
myself.

There may be a natural, healthy kind of fear, but the kind of fear I don't like and want not to obey is the fear that urges me to act contrary to my own feelings or to act before I know what my feelings are. It is usually a fear of displeasing other people. It is most often a fear of not doing what I (too quickly) *assume* others expect. I feel smaller, weaker and less a person after I have acted out of this kind of fear. I want to be aware of what others expect but not despotized by it. If I reflexively choose the opposite of what they expect I am still being controlled. What I want is to act out of love and respect for myself.

The way to be most helpful to others is for me to do the thing that right now would be most helpful to me.

I am not interested so much in what I do with my hands or words as what I do with my feelings. I want to live from the inside out, not from the outside in.

me too

Most words evolved as a description of
the outside world, hence their inadequacy
to describe what is going on inside me.

Wanting to do something is a desire, not
a sentence. When I "decide" what I want
to do I translate my desire into a sentence
and then follow the sentence; I take
the desire out of my body and put it in
my mind. Asking myself, "What do I
want to do?" brings to mind my habitual
answers to that question, it brings in
irrelevant things I "should" be wanting to
do, and it ignores the fact that there may
be no adequate words to describe what I
am feeling at *this* moment.

The configuration of most situations
implies, through tradition, a corresponding
emotion: e.g., your wife goes out on you
therefore you are enraged (when actually
you might be aroused). I often respond the
way I "should" feel rather than the way
I *do* feel. Confusion or indecision is a
good sign this is happening.

If I want to clarify what it is I want to
do about this situation then it would be
helpful for me to be certain I know the
difference between how I see these people
and how everyone is telling me they are.
I do not see Rudy as malicious. How do
I see him?—here I run into the problem
of how I really see him *at this time*
versus trying to remain consistent with
how I told everyone I saw him.

I can get more directly at what I am
really feeling if I think "I" instead of
"you" and stop talking to myself in the
third person. The third person postulates
an audience and so imposes a social "should."

Analysis is condemnation. I ask myself: "Why do you want to do that?" This question is malevolent. I am seeking a motive that I have already prejudged unworthy of me. Questioning my motives leads to a decision to thwart the desire I had. A healthier approach would be to accept the desire as mine and simply seek to learn its direction, seek to clarify it rather than judge it.

Most decisions, possibly all, have already
been made on some deeper level and my
going through a reasoning process to arrive
at them seems at least redundant. The
question, "What do I want to do?"
may often be a fearful reaction to the
subconscious decision I have already made.
It seems to be quite a different question
from: "What do I *really* want to do?" or,
better, "What am I really feeling?" These
questions acknowledge that at any given
moment I am experiencing a variety of
feelings and that what I want to do is
get at that one feeling which is most
central to me. If I can get in touch with
that then what to do will be obvious and
will probably follow naturally. On the
simplest level, if I feel, "I am thirsty," I
don't have to ask, "What do I want to do?"

Sometimes the only way for me to find
out what it is I want to do is to go
ahead and do something. Then the moment
I start to act, my feelings become clear.

Being myself includes taking risks with
myself, taking risks on new behavior,
trying new ways of "being myself," so
that I can see how it is I want to be.

If the desire to write is not accompanied
by actual writing then the desire is not
to write.

Standing before the refrigerator:
If I have to ask myself if I'm hungry,
I'm not.

... then, don't eat!

Someone asks: Would you like to do so-and-so? A picture forms in my mind and as I look at it, it is either appealing or unappealing and I say yes I would or no I wouldn't. But this picture is not precognitive, it is a composite of past experiences that will be more or less *unlike* the coming event.

I experience something in my life that is so tangible that I am puzzled as to why there is no word for it in English. Other people whom I have talked to also experience it, some more strongly than I. It is the feeling of "now is the time to do it." Often when I am asked why I haven't yet done something the answer is I haven't yet gotten this go-ahead. The astronauts receive a signal which comes closer to describing what I feel than anything else I have heard. It is: "All systems are GO."—But they can at least tell you where it's coming from.

My intuitive sense of the natural right thing to do under the circumstances, when it is really working, seems somehow to take future events into consideration. I feel, "Do this," and it is not until afterwards that I can see the sense of it.

To listen to my intuition is to identify with my entire awareness, to *be* my entire experience, and not just my conscious perception. My total awareness synthesizes into a calm sense of direction that is above reason.

It is only when my attention becomes fixated that I act like a part rather than a whole. When I favor my conscious perception over my total awareness, I can no longer hear the rhythm of the whole.

Calmness accompanies the whole. Fear accompanies the part. Intuition goes beyond the figure-ground focus of conscious perception.

It has been said that each of us is ultimately
alone. I prefer to think of now and here as
the only ultimate, but what is probably
meant is that our moments alone seem
somehow more true, more real. The word
"God" only begins to have meaning for me
when I am alone. It has no meaning for
me in a discussion. I don't think religion
is an attainable subject for the intellect.
I can only believe when I am not talking
about it.

I need solitude like I need food and rest,
and like eating and resting, solitude is most
satisfying when it fits the rhythm of my
needs. A regularly scheduled aloneness does
not nourish me.

Solitude is nearly a misnomer. To me,
being alone means togetherness—the re-coming-
together of me and nature, of me and being;
the reuniting of me with all. For me,
solitude especially means putting the parts
of me back together—the unifying of myself
whereby I see once again that the little
things are little and the big things are big.

I believe that solitude is a profound and
needed act of self-love and self-appreciation.

this, reminds me of you

When I was "religious" I at times got very frustrating results when I tried to constantly rely on my intuition to guide me. This suggests that I should use my intuition when I feel like it, use meditation when I feel like it, use reasoning when this feels natural, etc. It is absurdly self-contradictory to think I must always rely on my intuition because I have *reasoned out* that this is best.

For the last week I have been playing a game. I have been trying to predict what I would be doing in five minutes or in two minutes. I have found that no matter how hard I try I am more often wrong than right, and when I am right it is obvious that this outcome has been reached so precariously that the results seem accidental. I have also been struck with the radical difference between my fantasy about the future and the actual experience itself. My prediction is at most a vague picturing of a *category* of activity whereas the experience itself is made up of mood, thoughts, bodily sensations, detailed perceptions, etc., none of which are exactly like what I have experienced before. I have discovered that when I am aware of all of this (the radical unpredictability and unperceivability of the immediate future) I find it impossible to be bored. As I write this I am convinced that boredom is a false concept of the future. My boredom leans on my expectation that the immediate future will be "the same old thing." I cannot expect imminent change and remain bored.

I am noticing that when I am bored I
think I am tired of my surroundings but
I am really tired of my thoughts. It is
trite, repetitious, unobserved thinking that
is producing the discontent. Adopting a
quiet awareness, a kind of listening
attitude, usually freshens my mind and
brings the situation I am in to life.

i tried it.... and it works

If my attention is wandering, there is
somewhere it wants to go, so obviously it
does not want to be where I am holding
it in the name of some self-styled obligation.

... like in lectures

A plan eliminates boredom by promising change. But, ironically, a plan is only my decision to *imagine* a different future, and if followed too rigidly it precludes spontaneous happenings.

Sometimes my boredom works like this: I don't like what I am doing and I can't think of anything else to do, or what I do think of seems remote and impractical. My mind races from one unsatisfactory plan to another and my boredom deepens and I become increasingly frustrated. When this happens I find it helpful to suspend my efforts to "decide." Thinking that my intellect alone must choose makes my body into an object and splits me. But if I pause and become very aware of the flow of feelings going on inside me, I presently feel an impulse from within quietly directing me what to do, or I notice that I have already acted, and that "deciding" was not a part of it. Sometimes the "what to do" is to continue sitting.

It is not necessary to always think words. Words often keep me from acting in a fully intuitive way. Fears, indecision and frustration feed on words. Without words they usually stop. When I am trying to figure out how I should relate to some- one, especially a stranger, if I will stop thinking words, and listen to the situation, and just be open, I find I act in a more appropriate, more spontaneous, often original, sometimes even courageous way. Words are at times good for looking back, but they are confining when I need to act in the present.

When I'm critical of another person, when I see his behavior as a "fault," my attitude includes these feelings: I think of him as one thing (instead of having many parts). I dislike him. I "just can't understand" his action. He seems unjustified. And I think he "knows better." If I feel this way I am in reality seeing my own self-condemnation. "Fault" means failure to meet a standard. Whose? Mine. Another person's behavior is "bad" or "understandable" according to my experience with *myself*. My criticism of him amounts to: If I had said that or acted that way I would think of myself as selfish, opinionated, immature, etc. A part of me wants to act that way or thinks of myself as acting that way and condemns this. If I understood why I act like that, or want to, and had forgiven myself for it, I wouldn't be condemning this person now. I'm getting upset with him because there is something in me I don't understand and haven't yet accepted.

Simply because they had not paid all of
their rent, Lorson tried to get Mac and
Lore convicted of a felony. I feel disgust
for him. I consider him a sissy and a
weakling. He seems like something that
should be stepped on.

But if he had shot them what would I
have felt? Probably not anger; but a gangster
in my place might have felt anger. If
Lorson had cannibalized them I would not
have felt anger at all but shock, amazement
and possibly even a kind of pity for him.

The principle seems to be: It is a "fault"
if I am also capable of it, a disease if I
am not.

If I feel aversion toward someone, if I
find myself ignoring or turning away from
someone in a group, I am probably avoiding
within myself what this person represents
that is true about me.

If something that you do rankles me I
can know that your fault is my fault too.

The criticism that hurts the most is the
one that echoes my own self-condemnation.

I have two principal ways of discovering the areas where I fail to see myself. The first is acknowledging the qualities in others which irritate me. The second is recognizing the comments that make me defensive. All I have to do to discover what rankles me in other people's behavior is to review my latest encounters, but I have more difficulty recognizing when I am being defensive. I can identify it best by the following syndrome: I answer quickly. I feel in need of talking at length, and I feel impatient when interrupted. I explain. I try to persuade. But I feel frustrated even if I appear to succeed, as if the damage has already been done. I think hurriedly, and I feel a strong resistance to pausing and considering, as if something will be lost if I do this. My face feels fixed and serious. I usually avoid eye contact immediately after hearing the comment. I am incapable of taking the comment any way but seriously; the words never seem light or funny to me. When my reaction becomes apparent to the people present *they* often take the situation lightly. I feel somewhat misunderstood and misused.

Now that I know that when I criticize another
I am seeing my own fault I like to be very
honest and very *specific* in my criticism.
After I get it straight how I think this fault
works in someone else, I can then look at
my own behavior with a surprising new
clarity. (This way of criticizing works best
when I do it silently.)

When I feel defensive I like it best when I
remain aware of my defensiveness and yet
continue to act just as defensively as I
feel like acting.

No one is wrong. At most someone is un-
informed. If I think a man is wrong, either
I am unaware of something, or he is. So
unless I want to play a superiority game
I had best find out what he is looking at.

(interesting statement)

"You're wrong" means "I don't understand you"—I'm not seeing what you're
seeing. But there is nothing *wrong* with
you, you are simply not me and that's
not wrong.

I always seem to be feeling either superior
or inferior, one up or one down, better
off or worse off than everyone else. The
superior moments are elating, but the rare
and blessed moments are when I feel equal.

*these moments are indeed
unusual, and some
have been to you.*

There is no such thing as "best" in a
world of individuals.

Why this need to divide up, classify and neatly package every new acquaintance? For me to try to classify something so complex as an individual human being merely demonstrates my own shallowness. A judgement of another person is an abstraction that adds qualities that are not there and leaves out what is unique about him. If I classify someone I turn him into a thing. The only way for me to contact this other person is to experience him, not think about him.

This: It is such a chore to talk to Bill.
Why is he such a drag?

Versus this: I make such a chore for
myself when I talk to Bill. How do
I make it so hard?

The way to resolve this wish to share my
marital troubles with someone else and at
the same time remain loyal to Gayle is to
express them as mine and not as caused by her.

When Bruce said he had trouble getting
along with his mother, I liked him better.
I like a man with faults, especially when
he knows it! To err is human—I'm
uncomfortable around gods.

I have the choice of being right
or being human.

If I see someone I have been criticizing I
am usually especially nice to him.

It is impossible to make a general statement
that covers every exception, and yet
conversation so often consists of each
person pointing out the obvious exceptions
to the other person's statements.

i wonder why this is

I can't legitimately disagree with what you
say about yourself, only with what you
say about what is not yourself. The most
I can answer to what you say about
yourself is that I'm different.

The statements that communicate most
clearly are about me, you, now, here;
and all final authorities are present.

A generalization is an assertion that what
is true for me is also true for not-me.
I notice that I often talk in generalities to
produce the illusion that my "truth" is
shared. In this way I pick up a little
support (sameness) for my individualness
and don't feel so alone.

Sometimes when I generalize I am saying,
"Let's pretend I am God," and of course
the other person argues that point endlessly.
But I notice that if the other person
takes a stand for himself and states
his thoughts as *his* thoughts, I pay more
attention to what he is saying and look
deeper in myself.

If you tell me the way *you* see it rather
than the way it "is," then this helps me
to more fully discover the way I see it.

Whenever I find myself arguing for something with great passion, I can be certain
I'm not convinced. moi · aussi

I find it almost impossible to make a
strong declarative statement in conversation
without feeling little nagging doubts and
reservations.

"I agree" and "I disagree" are impossible
states of mind. No two people can think
exactly alike or antithetically. Sometimes
I say "I agree," because I want to avoid
an encounter; sometimes I just want to
get the other person to shut up. I usually say
"I disagree," when I want to exhibit myself.

There is an important difference between
telling a person how I experience him
and adding arguments to support the
correctness of my view. My feelings about
another do not require a case—I don't
notice them deductively.

When someone disagrees with me, I do not have to immediately start revising what I just said.

People don't want me to always agree with them. They can sense this is phony. They can sense I am trying to control them: I am agreeing with them to make them like me. They feel; "I don't want to exist to like you. I DON'T exist to like you."

Negative feedback is better than none. I would rather have a man hate me than overlook me. As long as he hates me I make a difference.

Raping, hunting, throwing stones at wildlife, buying exotic pets, picking flowers, criticizing prominent people, may at times be an attempt to make contact with, even identify with, that which is free and beautiful and so frightfully unlike us.

If someone criticizes me I am not any less because of that. It is not a criticism of me but critical thinking from him. He is expressing his thoughts and feelings, not my being.

Before, I thought I was actually fighting for my own self-worth; that is why I so desperately wanted people to like me. I thought their liking me was a comment on me, but it was a comment on them.

The question I could ask myself after receiving criticism is, "Does his statement give me any insight into myself?" not "Is it true?" If I say "That's true," those words really mean "I think about myself in the same way." No one knows whether or not it *is* true.

"What an ass I made of myself." —No,
I didn't make the impression. It was his
impression of me. I don't come across as
any one thing. I don't predetermine a set
reaction. There are any number of ways a
person can react to what I do. How he
chooses to react is his responsibility.
(This is a little harder to see if I
"make a big hit.")

I do not *have* to react to criticism with hurt feelings. It is my interpretation of *the meaning for me* that produces the pain. Bob says, "Sometimes you act like a three-year-old," or Esther says, "You sound like a preacher." What meaning do these comments have for me? I am the one who must choose to interpret them as derogatory; they are not inherently so. I am the one who must make the connection and call it bad. I believe that if I were more fully conscious and acceptant of the way I am, if I were more familiar with "me," I would not feel so criticized or complimented by people's words but would be confident to judge their accuracy for myself.

Insecurity can mean lack of self-knowledge:
I am not secure with myself—I can't rely
on myself—I don't know how I operate.
I am insecure to the degree I keep parts
of myself hidden from myself.
Or insecurity can mean I know how I
operate but don't think it's good enough.
When I find myself trying to figure out
beforehand how I should act (that is,
planning it out), this shows me I lack
respect for the way I am—I can't be
trusted to be perfect and so I have to
make rules. Otherwise I just might slip
and be a human being.

The need to "build myself up" is probably
what makes me, Paul, etc., talk excessively.
The fear that I'm not much prompts me
on because my experience tells me that
in the past the right words have wowed
people—"If I can just say the right words
these people will like me."

Bragging is a half-hidden, matter-of-fact
rehearsal of past accomplishments, that I
usually slip into the conversation under false
pretenses—as opposed to the excited sharing
of some recent recognition or achievement
with a friend.

Last night I started using swear words with Bill when I thought I was sounding nicer than I felt. Evidently I want to swear in order to become more real—or is it to sound more real?

When I swear, I am being something rather than saying something.

Profanity fixes the other person's attention on my words rather than my thoughts.

good point

It could be that if I were not afraid to
just "be me" I would be naturally funny.
It could be that a humorous response does
flick through my mind, but fear of what
people might think if I just blurted out
my thoughts kills it.

My saying "and" and "uh" results from
my need to answer immediately, to speak
without any break, as if taking time to
think were embarrassing.

Interpreting the pause is *their* problem.

F. S.
g 4
r t
e

If I feel compelled to answer every
question, *I* am the one compelling me.

Maybe I'd better not talk any more, they may be tired of listening to me. But I am talking because *I* want to, because it's doing something for *me*, not because it's doing something for them. So the question is do *I* want to talk some more.

I want to say something to this person but the fear comes: "I'd better not" (he may misunderstand, he may be in a hurry, ad infinitum). These fears are not based on the present situation, they are based on the past, and I don't have to be governed by what *once* went wrong. The two of us are standing here in the present. What is the situation *now*?

There is something about compliments that
scares me. Part of the reason may be that
I am afraid of getting something that can
subsequently be taken away. I put myself
in the hands of this other person if I let
my emotions lean on his statement.
Another reason: I am being put on the spot
and now must watch my actions to keep
him thinking this way about me. Another:
There is a part of me that knows I am
not as good as his compliment implies.
Another: I have often been insincere when
saying similar things.

Both Bill and Bob have accused me of
wanting to make them my father when I
have complimented them excessively. What
motivates me to blow up another person
bigger than life? Possibly it is because I
see this good and want it to be all-in-all.
I want to lose myself in it. I don't know
that it's bad, just excessive. It seems very
similar to becoming infatuated with a
beautiful woman.

The way to handle praise is honestly.
Laurel said, "You are one of the kindest
people I have ever known." I could have
said, "I believe I am kind but not as kind
as you see me. We have only known each
other a short time and I have been putting
my best foot forward. After you know me
better I believe you will agree I can be as
thoughtless as the next guy."

My friendship with Laurel seems to typify
a dialectic that many of my newly-forming
friendships go through. At first we saw
only each other's *virtues*. Now we are
seeing only each other's *faults*. If we
make it through this latter stage then
maybe we will see *each other* and
truly be friends.

true friends are a rare & precious thing

thanks...

for being one of these
special people

Sometimes my contacts with people are frustrating. Sometimes after I have been with someone I feel unsatisfied and slightly irritated, as if I have been wasting my time. This suggests to me now that these feelings arise from a thwarting of my expectations. I go wanting something from the person and do not get it. Things I might want: approval, help, fun, entertainment (escape from boredom), recognition, love, sex, justification.

If I need your approval I can't see you.

I need approval, but now that I'm no
longer a child I don't have to get it
from any one person.

this isn't true for me
approval from certain people
is still important . . .

am i still a child?

Dislike is a function of need. I want
something from you that you do not
provide and so I dislike that condition
and call you bad. The squirrel who lives
behind my cabin becomes furious whenever
I empty the garbage. I do not need his
approval and his anger amuses me. But if he
were my pet and I needed his cooperation
then this same anger would irritate me.
I do not dislike a stone unless it is in
my path, or a cloud unless it rains on
me. If I feel in need of something from
you then I hear your words only as yes,
no, maybe, or irritatingly off the subject.
I cannot appreciate you as you are and
cannot begin to see the world as you
see it.

Most conversations seem to be carried out on two levels, the verbal level and the emotional level. The verbal level contains those things which are socially acceptable to say, but it is used as a means of satisfying emotional needs. Yesterday a friend related something that someone had done to her. I told her why I thought the person had acted the way he had and she became very upset and started arguing with me. Now, the reason is clear. I had been listening to her words and had paid no attention to her feelings. Her words had described how terribly this other person had treated her, but her emotions had been saying, "Please understand how I felt. Please accept my feeling the way I did." The last thing she wanted to hear from me was an explanation of the other person's behavior.

I talk because I feel, and I talk to you
because I want you to know how I feel.

My statements are requests.

My questions are statements.

My trivia is an invitation to be friends.

My gossip is a plea: Please see me as
incapable of that. Please respect me.

My arguments insist: I want you to show
respect for me by agreeing with me. This
is the way *I* say it is.

And my criticism informs you: You hurt
my feelings a minute ago.

not necessarily

If I ignore the emotional plea and
respond only to the words, I will not be
communicating with you, there will not
be a flow of understanding between us, I
will not be feeling you and so I will be
frustrated and you will be also. The heart of
any conversation is the demand being made
on my emotions. If I feel frustrated, that
is a good sign I am avoiding the emotions
you are trying to communicate—I have not
paused long enough to ask, "What do you
really want from me?"

important for "Care givers" to respond
like this

I don't want to listen to just what you
say. I want to feel what you mean.

I won't hold you to your words. Deep
emotions are often expressed in irrational words.

Boy - that's the truth!

I want you to be able to say anything.

i'll listen

Even what you don't mean.

I am afraid of your silence because of what
it could mean. I suspect your silence of
meaning you are getting bored or losing
interest or making up your own mind
about me without my guidance. I believe
that as long as I keep you talking I can
know what you are thinking. *i used to feel this way c you—*
but i dont anymore

But silence can also mean confidence. And
mutual respect. Silence can mean live and
let live: the appreciation that I am I and
you are you. This silence is an affirmation
that we are already together—as two people.
Words can mean that I want to make you
into a friend and silence can mean that I
accept your already being one.

you ... are one of few people I
communicate with in silence
and feel totally at ease.

My experience indicates that blunt honesty
with my feelings gives me greater empathy
with other people's feelings. My feelings
appear to be a truer register of another
person's feelings than my intellect. To
better get at what is going on in him
I sometimes ask myself not, "What is
happening in him?" but "What do *I feel* is
happening in him?" In order to see more
clearly what he is feeling I at times have
to stop listening to what he is saying, and
what I am thinking, and look inside
myself. Then if I speak from this feeling
within, and tell him what *I* understand
him to be saying, he will usually set me
straight if I have not got it right.

I must do these things in order to communicate: Become aware of you (discover you). Make you aware of me (uncover myself). Be ready to change during our conversation, and be willing to reveal my changes to you.

For communication to have meaning it must have a life. It must transcend "you and me" and become "us." If I truly communicate, I see in you a life that is not me and partake of it. And you see and partake of me. In a small way we then grow out of our old selves and become something new. To have this kind of sharing I cannot enter a conversation clutching myself. I must enter it with loose boundaries. I must give myself to the *relationship*, and be willing to be what grows out of it.

"Talking at" and "talking about" appear to be communication but are not. Gayle and I "talk about" when we go over to another couple's house and all evening the only thing said is, "Yes, and isn't it so," as if the rule were to quickly find something outside ourselves to talk about that we can all agree on is terrible. The only personal comments are made while we are driving home.

Two ways I have of talking "at" the other person instead of "with" him are: Talking in order to seduce him into thinking I am right, and talking in order to sound right to myself.

Last night I suddenly realized that each of
us was wasting much energy trying to
relate what we wanted to say to what the
last person had just said. A funny "should"!
I see now that I was not always honest
when I did this. Often I could not tell
what connection had been made inside me
that resulted in my wanting to say what
I did, so I would manufacture a relationship
to the discussion in order to be able to
tell everyone a good reason for my wanting
to talk. The reason was simply that I wanted
to. "I want to say such-and-such—" not
"What you said raises this question—"

If I want to communicate with you I must keep you informed of my feelings. A question often hides my feelings. It is sometimes my attempt to discover your position before I reveal mine, or it sometimes hides a criticism I don't want to risk stating. If I ask you, "Why do you say that?" or "Is that what you really think?" I show you little of what I am feeling. Instead I put you on the defensive without making clear what it is in me I want you to respond to.

The more abstract the question you ask me ("Are you really happy? Do you love mankind?—Your country?—God?"), the more impossible I find it is for me to get in touch with *any feeling at all.*

I experience the feelings that make me want to open my mouth and speak, not as questions but as demands. My words spring from my emotions and my emotions are declarative, not interrogative. Even my feeling of curiosity is a statement of what I want.

"You ought to" means "I want you to,"
so why not say so?

When I say "you should," I avoid
committing myself. I am referring you
to some supposedly objective standard and
saying that circumstances or decency or
what-have-you dictates that you do this,
while I pretend to stay out of it.

But if I make you aware of just how I
feel, your reaction might give me much
blunt information about myself—or at
least about *us*.

"Let's not get personal"—Unless what you say relates to me as a person it is just words without meaning. But let's not just get personal about each other, let's get personal about ourselves.

Whether written or spoken, the more intensely personal, the more uniquely applicable to *him* a man's thoughts are, the more I find that what he says has meaning for me. There is usually more meat for me in a writer's journals than in his essays.

Many people think they are acting the way they feel when they tell someone off. Someone is critical of me and I answer by calling him an S.O.B. My feeling is not that he is an S.O.B.; my feeling is that he has hurt me: "You have hurt my feelings and now I want to hurt yours." Launching a verbal attack covers up my feeling of being hurt with an appearance of strength. I get angry when I think someone has hurt me in a way I am helpless to do anything about.

I get angry at Gayle when she asks me to do something if I sense that in refusing to do what she asks I will demonstrate that I am not the way I like to think of myself.

Is there a healthy anger? When I defend myself against an assault designed to destroy me—that's healthy anger. When I attack a man because he reminds me of a rejected part of me—try to blot out that image of myself and take him down with it, then that anger is unhealthy.

But why can I easily get angry at Gayle and not even *feel* it toward my boss, who constantly abuses me? I must be afraid of losing something and so turn on myself to undercut the aggression. He berates me and I immediately start seeing "truth" in his criticism and so become the only weapon that can harm me.

Morbid self-doubt destroys anger. I experience my healthy anger as a response to what I see him as doing, but it is more accurately a rebellion against what I am doing to myself. This good anger springs from self-respect and unites me. It tells me where I am and asserts my right to be there. My healthy anger is my willingness to be conscious, and to be seen, and to be emphatically myself.

I'm glad that Gayle trusts me and our
relationship enough to be able to occasionally
blow up at me.

Our marriage used to suffer from arguments
that were too short. Now we argue long
enough to find out what the argument
is about.

I can get along with people a lot better
if I realize that no one ever feels exactly
the same about me or anyone else from
one moment to the next. And, likewise,
it is self-destructive to believe *I* must
love anyone all of the time.

Esther may dislike me from time to time
and I want to respect that by not trying
to quickly change her feelings as if they
were wrong.

If we do not exist as individuals then our
relationship does not exist. *c'est vrai!*

"All I want is for you to accept me
as I am."

"Yes, and all *I* want is for you to accept
my not accepting you." *that's hard to swallow*

I can't assume that this woman wants sex with me simply because I want sex with her, but I can open my eyes and see if she does and take a reasonable risk and ask her—without trying to predetermine her answer by the way I phrase the question.

If she could choose any man she wanted she would probably not choose me, but I have been strongly attracted to many women who were far from ideal and knew it. The question is not how do I compare with all men. The question is am I sexually attractive to *this* woman at *this* time. "Am I sexy as hell, or too fat?"— that can't be answered, but "How is she experiencing me?" can be. To get the answer I have to look to her and not at me.

If my sexual desire for a woman is so strong and so persistent that it is getting in the way of my communication with her, then I might do her, and me, a favor by telling her so. I have done this several times in my life and each time I felt the woman appreciated it (although once the husband did not). Some surprised me by saying they felt the same way, some said they did not feel that way about me, one woman did not say. But in all the instances except the last our communication seemed much freer afterwards.

I feel sensually attracted to Leah as she
walks in the door with Bill. Now, if I
am open, if I broaden my awareness to
include Bill's presence, Gayle's presence, my
emotions, etc., then my response will be
in rhythm with the situation as a whole.
It is only when I am mentally myopic
that my actions become excessive or restricted.

I don't like the way I acted toward Alice.
I was experiencing her as a very attractive
woman, and yet the whole time I acted like
an asexual nice-guy. When I feel like a man
I want to act like one and not like a
polite eunuch.

You say you just want to be my friend.
I know you mean you want to relate to
my mind but not to my body. I can
understand that, and will not ask you to
relate to me in a way you don't want to.
But likewise I refuse to castrate myself
for you by pretending. If you want to
have me as your friend you will have to
accept my penis along with me.

What is the difference between "I want
food" and "I want sex"?

Consent.

Let's say I want sex with a woman. If
she doesn't want sex with me and I allow
myself to accept this fact completely
then I will probably no longer want her
in that way either.

But I doubt it.

"I just can't write her off."—It's not that. It's that I can't admit my uselessness to her, I can't allow myself to be written out of *her* life.

"All I want is to be loved."—Wanting to be loved, to be lovable, is not really a desire for how I want to be, but for how I want others to be.

"I need your heart and your eyes and your ears and your touch and your words. I want you to see me and hear me and feel me and speak to me and love me." But by giving what I want, I realize that I have what I thought I lacked before.

Several months ago I discovered that I was interpreting a particular sensation in my abdomen as "hunger" which, when I listened more closely, turned out to be "tension." Now when I have this feeling I like breathing deeply and stretching my back better than going to the refrigerator. When I was in Berkeley I experienced very powerful sensations which I interpreted as a desire for sex. Later I became close friends with several women but didn't have sex with them, and these feelings lessened. Maybe the feelings were more a desire for companionship than sex partners. But now I am in the mountains and am alone much of the time and the feelings have gone altogether (almost). It is equally logical for me to assume that in Berkeley what I really longed for was solitude. But I think the better answer is that feelings are not words ("tension," "hunger," "loneliness"). Feelings are sensations, and no two feelings are ever quite identical.

I don't *feel* "I want." I feel "I lack."
I *decide* "I want."

I am more careful now when I make the
jump from "I feel" to "I want." I see
now that this jump is the difference
between feeling a lack and deciding best
how to fill it. The more closely I listen
to the particular sensations I am having
at the moment, the more satisfactorily
I can decide what word to call them and
what action to take. Sometimes the feeling
turns out not to be a "lack" at all.

While I am worrying about what you think of me I am not open to you, I am not letting you in; in fact, I am not letting you exist as a person—I am making you my mirror. While I am concerned with what you are thinking about me I am not even thinking about you.

I choose to use my own mind. I do not need your mind. I want to experience you, listen to you—not to myself. I have already heard everything I have to say. You are what is novel about this conversation.

In order to see I have to be willing to be seen. *this can be scarey*

If a man takes off his sunglasses I can hear him better.

As long as I'm giving you things (even "love") I don't have to notice you.

i don't agree c̄ this
to me, love is giving of yourself
mind
body
& soul

"I don't care what people think"—that is the most dishonest sentence in the English language. I say it because I want to believe I don't care what people think, or I want you to.

What matters is not the caring but the *way* that I care. Spending all morning in the bathroom is not really caring what people think; it is in fact an unwillingness to let people think. The attention I give to what I wear, the length of my hair, how much I weigh, etc., is designed to *control* what people will think.

And if I don't keep the curtains closed, you might catch me off guard and make up your own mind!

I used to dislike social functions to the
point that I considered myself a sincere
misanthrope. What I didn't realize was that
I hated having to shield myself, the hard
and unpleasant work of acting without
acknowledging it. Now that I feel freer
to let myself alone and allow others to
like or dislike me as they choose, I have
lost much of this aversion to socializing.

One must be a courageous
person to do this

I learn most about myself by observing
myself in relation to others. When I
examine myself by myself I am actually
examining the results of a previous encounter.

Perceptions are not of things but of
relationships. Nothing, including me,
exists by itself—this is an illusion of words.
I *am* a relationship, ever-changing.

I walk down the street and the guy
waiting for the bus—who has been waiting
there for God knows how long—suddenly
finds something more interesting to look
at than a live human being. I do the same.

Do I avoid looking a stranger in the
eyes because I don't want to make him
uncomfortable, or do I turn my eyes so
he can't look into me?

What is there in me that I don't want
him to see?

Something within me will not let me rest
with a bad opinion of another person.
Dislike is for me an unpleasant sensation.
It distresses me to hear someone criticize
another person he knows, and I feel uneasy
when I join in. Hatred seems to be its
own punishment, but something in me
rejoices in a new-found appreciation. As
an act of faith, as a response to something
that feels very deep in me, I believe this
about another human being: Regardless of
his present mood (and I want to respect
that, whatever it is) he wants to be my
friend. For no other reason than I am
also a human being, he wants to feel love
for me and wants me to feel love for him.
Deep within him he wants us to be close.

One thing has become quite clear: all
acquaintances are passing. Therefore I want
to make the most of every contact. I
want to quickly get close to the people
I meet because my experience has shown
we won't be together long.

i've met many people i would like
to have known better

but friends need not always be together
it's the feeling of closeness
when you're apart
that proves a lasting relationship

How much do I really love *people*? If I had been cut off from people for 20 or 30 years—totally cut off—I would love to hear the yelling upstairs, the screaming of the children, the barking dog, the loud record player. I would not want it all shut off as I went to sleep, but would savor it even as I dozed off.

I love people when I love them for being
people, and not for being young or old
or beautiful or hip. I wish I could love
what man has built just because man has
built it: streets, telephone poles, buildings,
cars. It is easy to love nature. Why? I
have been taught that nature is lovable.
But form, rhythm, grace, melody, color
are subjective. Why isn't traffic music to
me, and music noise?

I love myself when I am myself.

Love unites the part with the whole.
Love unites me with the world and with
myself. My life work could well be love.
Love is the universe complete. Detachment
is the universe divided. Detachment divides
me from myself and from others. Love is
the vision that can see all as one and one
as all: "I and my father are one." Is
there but one reality and one truth? Love
shows me where all minds and essences unite.

How do I get love? I have it. I must
drop my definitions of love. Love is not
saying nice things to people or smiling or
doing good deeds. Love is love. Don't
strive for love, be it.

I love because I love.

There is a certain beauty in poverty, loss
and desolation. There is a certain strength
and grandeur in suffering. Grays, storms,
ruins, age are powerful subjects for a painting.
Even a dump heap can evoke admiration.

It is not that there is no evil, accidents, deformity, pettiness, hatred. It's that there *is* a broader view. Evil exists in the part. Perfection exists in the whole. Discord is seeing near-sightedly. And I can choose this broader view—not that I always *should*—but I always *can*.

Ideas are clean. They soar in the serene
supernal. I can take them out and look
at them, they fit in books, they lead
me down that narrow way. And in the
morning they are there. Ideas are straight—

But the world is round, and a
messy mortal is my friend.

Come walk with me in the mud. . . . .

in the sand
č the waves chasing
your toes

To the reader:

I enjoyed writing this book, but now I am feeling some limitations in it, and I want you to know my reservations.

First, my notes sometimes sound like axioms, and I don't like this. I can't think of a lasting truth in the form of a statement that I have ever heard or read; why then should *I* be able to make one? Some statements have come back to me from time to time, and some that had little meaning when I ingested them, later surfaced with surprising force; but there are none that have retained a constant value for me.

Second, I keep thinking of exceptions to what I have written; or maybe they are additions, maybe both are true. For example, last night I heard myself say to a man, "Let's not get personal," in apparent contradiction to what I had written in one of my notes. What a part of me had come to realize was that my style of being congruent just wasn't working with this person. But he took this mild reprimand, and even called himself on it several times afterwards. A strictly abstract discussion followed and lasted for several hours. It greatly pleased him, and it brought us closer together than we had ever been.

My third point concerns the times in this book I speak of my choosing the positive in me to act on instead of the negative. That sounded good when I wrote it, but frankly I don't experience "choice," "decision" and "will" as the neat packages their names imply. "I decide" suggests a starting point, a spontaneous creation, whereas what I experience within me is more a flow, a flow that has always been going on. I flow in one direction and not in another, and as I notice this direction I say to myself, "I have decided." If choice were in reality the selecting of one part of me over another then my decisions would divide me and alienate the unchosen parts. What I see in my life is an ever-deepening awareness that unites me as it goes to the core of me. My awareness deepens *and* my behavior (what I call in this book "choices") becomes more positive. I experience depth of awareness and degree of positiveness as one thing. "Choice" implies that they are separate and so makes the "will" appear more important than it is.

The fourth point is that I keep seeing a "higher truth," and this disturbs my sense of having completed this book. For example, I talk about accepting my feelings and not condemning myself for the negative ones, but I am wondering now if my negative feelings are not equally as valuable as my positive ones. Certainly it is true that all along my category of negative feelings has been shrinking. I now see new usefulness in grief, worry, doubt and suffering. In this book I talk about how boredom has sometimes motivated me to creativity. I recently found that tiredness can be a delicious feeling if I value it. And a few weeks ago I discovered that by appreciating a feeling of revenge I got in touch with my compassion. It happened like this: After receiving a great deal of (what seemed to me to be) malicious criticism from a man, I found that I was having many spontaneous revenge fantasies. I tried to accept these but felt I was stuck and that nothing productive was happening. Then it occurred to me to do something more than just accept my fantasies. I tried going with them. I tried to enjoy them and to make them even bigger and better. And a surprising thing happened. After I had created a particularly violent ending to a fantasy, I suddenly saw this person in an entirely new light—I saw his side—and I felt an understanding and warmth for him I had not experienced before.

I am no longer so sure that love is *the* greatest thing in the world, that it is any better for me or for those to whom I express it than, say, anger. Other people's anger has done a hell of a lot for me: I don't think I would choose to have those moments replaced by love. Faith in what is happening inside me seems a healthier attitude than discrimination. If there is any good in the world I am beginning to think that I have to first see it in me, and the more I look the more I am finding that *whatever* I feel is exactly right for me.

Now if it is true—and I am not yet sure that it is—that I will come to appreciate, even want, all of my feelings no matter what they are, and not just accept them, then I need to rewrite much of this book. But if I do that, of course I will no longer be in the same situation I am in now, and as the situation changes the thoughts which are helpful to me will change with it. The answer must be for me to use an idea as long as it is usable and not be afraid to let go of it when it has served its purpose. Thoughts and books, sometimes great religions and certain people, provide me with a broader view, but then I feel a familiar malaise and I know that the time has come for me to move on, maybe someday to return, maybe not.

The fifth point I want to make is that the kind of writing I have done in this book is usually an expression of insights on my current *problems*. As I write I am in a state of learning, becoming, arriving, and not in a state of knowing and having arrived. I write about communication because I find it hard to talk to people. I write about my sexual desires because I am learning to cope with them. Therefore what I have written here is of necessity imperfect and halting—a grasping for truth and not truth. I notice that I sometimes use superlatives to impress a new discovery on me like a child beating his head "to get it through his thick skull." I sometimes use generalizations in the same way, or sometimes to broaden the hegemony of my "truth," or sometimes to convince you—to cause you to accept my truth for yours, and thereby gain the illusion of expanding my self. Often writing serves the same purpose for me as arguing—a testing to see if the ideas can bear scrutiny, but at times it goes even further and is a cry for help.

As I write this I am feeling that this last point I want to make is the most important one. I have seen "being real" act sometimes like a new kind of religion, a new form of self-justification, a new perfectionism, or even a perverse new snobbery. I experienced this recently when I found myself arguing against someone else's truth on the grounds that his truth professed to be universal whereas *I knew* all truth to be personal. I was in effect shouting down his throat: "You shouldn't be telling me what I shouldn't be."—or—"I won't accept your not believing in acceptance." I also sense that I am misusing the idea of being real whenever I discover myself anxiously weighing my words and actions, that is, whenever I am being very careful to be "real." When I do this I am only playing a new role—the role of the "real person." Calculation does not enter into being real. Concern with appearances does not enter into it. Being real is more a process of letting go than it is the effort of becoming. I don't really have to become me, although at times it feels this way—I am already me. And that is both the easiest and the hardest thing for me to realize.

Hugh Prather
July, 1970
Chama, New Mexico